PRESENTED TO

_____

PRESENTED BY

_____

DATE

PROVERBS
FOR LIFE™

for Teens

Y
inspirio™

Proverbs for Life™ for Teens
ISBN 0-310-80179-6

Copyright © 2003 by GRQ Ink, Inc.
Franklin, Tennessee 37067
"Proverbs for Life" is a trademark owned by GRQ, Inc.

Published by Inspirio™, The gift group of Zondervan
5300 Patterson Avenue, SE
Grand Rapids, Michigan 49530

Requests for information should be addressed to:
Inspirio™, The gift group of Zondervan
Grand Rapids, Michigan 49530
http://www.inspiriogifts.com

Compiler: Lila Empson
Associate Editor: Janice Jacobson
Project Manager: Tom Dean
Manuscript written by Vicki J. Kuyper in conjunction with
    Snapdragon Editorial Group, Inc.
Design: Whisner Design Group

GET ALL THE ADVICE YOU CAN,

AND YOU WILL SUCCEED;

WITHOUT IT YOU WILL FAIL.

PROVERBS 15:22 GNT

Contents

Introduction

The book of Proverbs contains the timeless wisdom each person needs to live a happy, healthy, well-balanced life. Each entry teaches a practical principle designed to encourage good choices and positive problem solving.

Proverbs for Life™ for Teens takes those valuable principles and applies them to the issues teens care about most, such as friendship, loyalty, dealing with parents, and pursuing dreams. As you read through these pages, may you find the practical answers—God's answers—to the questions you are asking during this exciting period of your life.

Commit to the LORD everything you do. Then your plans will succeed.

— *Proverbs 16:3 NIRV*

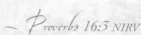

The Triumphant Heart

High atop the mountain
That now above me stands,
I see my goal quite clearly,
The object of my plans.

Each step I take brings triumph,
I consider no retreat.
For each and every victory
Takes me closer to the peak.

Anna O'Connor

Watching the Mouth

It is better to win control over yourself than over whole cities.

~ *Proverbs* 16:32 GNT

SAVE YOUR
BREATH TO
COOL YOUR
PORRIDGE.
—ENGLISH
PROVERB

Cassie was at it again, in a war of words—with a teacher no less. "Cassie, take your seat. I've asked you twice to be quiet," Mr. Doenges answered back, his eyebrows knit together in his trademark look of exasperation.

"But it's not fair. Other people used the same format I did and you didn't give them a *C*." Cassie shot back. Then, just like that, it was over. Cassie found herself on the way to the principal's office without having accomplished a thing. Her grade remained unchanged.

"All that work for nothing," Cassie muttered as she shuffled down the deserted hallway.

Then, Cassie remembered what her friend Cindi had told her about a thousand times. "Stop and think before you speak. Your mouth is always getting you in trouble." Cindi was right, and Cassie knew it. It was time for a change. She would start watching her mouth and would start thinking before she opened it.

Life is full of situations that can leave you feeling angry and frustrated, but responding to them emotionally by blurting out the first thing that pops into your head almost always makes things worse, not better. Waiting for the right time and place to present your case calmly and respectfully is the only way to have your concerns taken seriously. It's not easy to stay cool when tempers are running hot, but in the end it's the wise thing to do.

TRY THIS: *When you feel ready to let lose a string of angry words, stop and take a deep breath. Remind yourself that God has given you absolute control over what comes out of your mouth. Ask God to help you deal with your emotions and identify the right time and place to respond wisely to the situation.*

Not only to say the right thing in the right place, but far more difficult, to leave unsaid the wrong thing at the tempting moment.

GEORGE SALA

FUMBLE

Pride only breeds quarrels, but wisdom is found in those who take advice.

~ Proverbs 13:10 NIV

Greg was the best football player Jefferson High had ever seen. He knew it, his coaches knew it, the other players knew it—everybody knew it.

In Greg's mind, his future was a sure thing—football scholarship, then draft by the NFL, followed by fame and product endorsement contracts. Only one thing was standing in the way of Greg's inevitable rise to the top—chemistry.

Greg couldn't think of even one good reason to memorize a bunch of useless formulas. He'd been back and forth with his teacher, Mr. Diehl, trying to explain how utterly useless it would be to have him kicked off the team because of a poor chemistry grade. Apparently, Mr. Diehl didn't understand how important Greg was to the football team.

When Greg got to practice on the day after mid-term grades went out, he was pretty surprised to learn he would not be playing football for the rest of the season.

Greg couldn't see it, but the greatest threat to his success was not chemistry—it was pride. He was blinded by it, so much so that he thought he was too important to abide by the rules. Each of us has been given a special talent or skill. Don't let pride get in the way of your future success. Be humble, listen to advice, and become wise.

TRY THIS: *Look up the word pride. Among the several definitions offered, two are of special interest here. One type of pride "reflects credit upon oneself," but another reflects an "inordinate opinion of one's own importance." Write these meanings on an index card, read them often, and let God speak to you.*

WITH THE HUMBLE IS WISDOM.

PROVERBS 11:2 NIV

A MAN'S PRIDE BRINGS HIM LOW, BUT A MAN OF LOWLY SPIRIT GAINS HONOR.

PROVERBS 29:23 NIV

God sends no one away empty except those who are full of themselves.

DWIGHT L. MOODY

God's Gift to Me

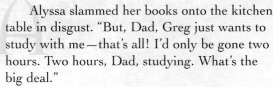

Listen to your father, who gave you life, and do not despise your mother when she is old.

— *Proverbs 23:22* NIV

Alyssa slammed her books onto the kitchen table in disgust. "But, Dad, Greg just wants to study with me—that's all! I'd only be gone two hours. Two hours, Dad, studying. What's the big deal."

"We hardly know Greg, and his parents aren't going to be home," Alyssa's dad responded. "That may not be a big deal to you, but it sure is to me. God made it my job to watch out for you, and I take that seriously."

Alyssa huffed off to her room. But as she sat in the quiet, she began to think about what her father had said—not about Greg, but about it being his job to protect her. Would she honestly want it any other way? Her parents weren't perfect, but she knew they loved her and did their best to care for her.

"Thanks, Lord, for my Mom and Dad," Alyssa whispered. "Help me to remember that they only want what's best for me."

Are you eager to start making your own choices and choosing your own path? If so, you're a normal teen, struggling with issues of freedom and independence. Just remember God has given you valuable allies to help you find your way along the path to adulthood. It doesn't make sense to fight against the very people to whom God has committed the responsibility of your care. They're God's gift to you.

Try this: Start a notebook to record the advice your parents give you, whether you agree with it or not. Example: "Don't wait until the last minute." Write everything down, including your initial reactions and later reflections. Read through your entire notebook in thirty days and record new comments. Note whether your opinion of the advice has changed and if it now seems like good information.

"RESPECT YOUR FATHER AND MOTHER" IS THE FIRST COMMANDMENT.

EPHESIANS 6:2 GNT

IT IS FOOLISH TO IGNORE WHAT YOUR PARENTS TAUGHT YOU; IT IS WISE TO ACCEPT THEIR CORRECTION.

PROVERBS 15:5 GNT

You will never be the person you can be if pressure, tension, and discipline are taken out of your life.

JAMES G. BILKEY

Turning Back

You are the one who will profit if you have wisdom.

~ Proverbs 9:12 GNT

Brandon wasn't quite sure how he'd gotten himself into this situation, but here he was, waiting in line to get his tongue pierced. It started out as one of those I'll-do-it-if-you-do-it dares between friends. He couldn't back out now. His friends would never let him forget it.

Brandon knew his mother would be angry. *She'll never understand. Why can't she see I'm old enough to decide for myself?* he thought. Then it hit him. This hadn't been his idea at all, and it certainly was not what he wanted. If he really was old enough to make his own decisions, then he was old enough to say no to his friends.

"Who's next?" said the young woman behind the counter. Brandon looked up and hesitated. Then he stepped out of line and headed for the door. Brandon left the shop comfortable with his decision.

It isn't easy to find your own voice in the midst of the crowd. It takes courage and maturity. But you will never be your own person as long as you let other people pull you along the path of life. Instead, let God help you make good choices. Since he created you, he is the only one who truly understands what will make you happy and successful.

TRY THIS: *Have a heart-to-heart chat with your parents. Ask them a few honest questions. For example, is there anything you wanted to do as a teenager that your parents wouldn't let you do? Do you have any regrets about choices you made during your teenage years? Consider how their feelings then might be similar to yours now.*

SENSIBLE PEOPLE ALWAYS THINK BEFORE THEY ACT.

PROVERBS 13:16 GNT

PAY ATTENTION TO WHAT YOU ARE TAUGHT, AND YOU WILL BE SUCCESSFUL.

PROVERBS 16:20 GNT

When you have to make a choice and don't make it, that in itself is a choice.

WILLIAM JAMES

The Honest Heart

When I present myself
as something I'm really not
I not only deceive others
I deceive myself.
But when I honestly face my fears
and own up to my mistakes,
I find the courage to become
The person God created me to be.

Tara Afriat

A lie has a short life,
but truth lives on forever.

— *Proverbs 12:19* GNT

Honest people are safe
and secure, but the
dishonest will be caught.

— *Proverbs 10:9* GNT

HONESTY IS THE
FIRST CHAPTER IN
THE BOOK OF
WISDOM.

THOMAS JEFFERSON

Sticking to the Plan

Commit to the LORD whatever you do, and your plans will succeed.

— Proverbs 16:3 NIV

PERSISTENT
PEOPLE BEGIN
THEIR SUCCESS
WHERE OTHERS
END IN FAILURE.
—EDWARD
EGGLESTON

This has to be a mistake. There's no way I didn't make the track team, Kate thought, taking a second look at the list posted outside the gym. Kate had been one of fastest sprinters on the middle school's track team, and she had the awards to prove it. But now Kate was in high school.

Holding back a wave of tears, Kate's eyes wandered to the bottom of the list. Her name was there after all—under ALTERNATE. "Forget this," Kate muttered to herself, hurrying off to her locker. Kate had put her time in for the last three years. She wasn't starting over. She'd quit the team.

Just then, Meghan, Central High's senior track star, caught sight of Kate. "Congratulations on making alternate," Meagan said with a smile. "It took me two years to make the team. See you Monday at practice."

Kate paused. *Maybe you will,* she thought. *Maybe you will.*

20

When God created you, he gave you gifts that are uniquely yours. Developing those talents and skills is up to you. Do you think you walked across the room the very first time you got up from crawling? No way. Chances are you fell a few times before you made it across the room. Life includes successes and failures, starts and stops, second chances and hard knocks. The key is not to give up—you will succeed if you keep on trying.

Try this: Tonight, try to eat dinner with your left hand. (If you're left-handed, use your right hand.) Practice this new "skill" every night for a week. Did it get easier as the week drew to a close? The next time you don't succeed at something the first time, remember how much difference just a week of trying can make. Don't give up.

IF WE DO NOT GIVE UP, THE TIME WILL COME WHEN WE WILL REAP THE HARVEST.

GALATIANS 6:9 GNT

TRUST IN THE LORD WITH ALL YOUR HEART, AND LEAN NOT ON YOUR OWN UNDERSTANDING.

PROVERBS 3:5 NIV

Permanence, perseverance and persistence in spite of all obstacles, discouragements, and impossibilities: It is this that in all things distinguishes the strong soul from the weak.

THOMAS CARLYLE

Investing in Others

A friend loves at all times.

~ *Proverbs 17:17 NASB*

How does a friendship start? You take a risk. You strike up a conversation with the new kid in class. You lend a quarter to the guy in line at the snack bar. You ask a question, give a compliment, or share a joke. You invest your time and interest in someone else's life.

How does a friendship end? You speak a careless word. You have a laugh at someone else's expense. You yield to pressure from peers to stop hanging out with losers. You love yourself more than you love someone you call friend.

Friends aren't outfits you choose to wear as long as they're in style or make you look good. Friendship is a keepsake that continues to grow more beautiful and more valuable with every passing season. But becoming "forever friends" doesn't happen on its own. It takes work. And sometimes, that work is anything but easy.

Real love, which is at the heart of any true friendship, means more than just enjoying another person's company. It means accepting others the way they are, while being honest enough to help them become the best they can be. It means forgiving them when they let you down, apologizing when you're at fault, and taking time to listen, even when you have something really important to say. It means caring more about what you can give than what you're going to get.

Try this: The next time you get together with a friend, think of your time as a gift to that person. What can you do to encourage, compliment, support, or help your friend? Put your own news on the back burner for the moment and really listen. Your friendship will surely grow.

WOUNDS FROM A FRIEND CAN BE TRUSTED.

PROVERBS 27:6 NIV

SOME FRIENDS ARE MORE LOYAL THAN BROTHERS.

PROVERBS 18:24 GNT

To have a good friend is one of the highest delights of life; to be a good friend is one of the noblest and most difficult undertakings.

AUTHOR UNKNOWN

Listen up

If you refuse good advice, you are asking for trouble; follow it and you are safe.

~ *Proverbs* 13:13 GNT

MANY RECEIVE
ADVICE, ONLY
THE WISE PROFIT
BY IT.
—SYRUS

Caleb loved to spend time with his grandfather and not just because he could clean a fish faster than anyone Caleb had ever seen. However, when they went fishing, Caleb felt that no matter what he said, his grandfather had some piece of "sound" advice he just couldn't wait to dish out:

"Bad company corrupts good character." "The love of money is the root of all evil." "Man does not live by bread alone." "The borrower is servant to the lender." "A cheerful heart is good medicine."

But when Caleb listened to his friend Brian brag about taking money from his girlfriend's purse so he could act like he was treating her to a movie after school, Caleb found his grandfather's words echoing in his head: "As water reflects a face, so a man's heart reflects the man" (Proverbs 27:19 NIV). Maybe there was some truth to his grandfather's words after all.

There are two ways to learn a lesson: the hard way—through personal experience—and the easy way—by listening to advice from people who learned their lesson the hard way. Not all advice is good advice, but if the person who's handing it out is someone you respect, and who has the experience behind him to back up his words, he may be worth listening to. Think of someone you know whose words of wisdom might make your life a little easier.

TRY THIS: *Try rewriting a few proverbs. For instance, for Proverbs 13:13 you could write, "Taking the advice of a wise person can be as refreshing as a cool water on a hot day. Acting on what I hear means I won't crash and burn." Rewriting is an effective memory device that will help you retain the wisdom you read.*

THE WAY OF A FOOL SEEMS RIGHT TO HIM, BUT A WISE MAN LISTENS TO ADVICE.

PROVERBS 12:15 NIV

GET ALL THE ADVICE YOU CAN, AND YOU WILL SUCCEED; WITHOUT IT YOU WILL FAIL.

PROVERBS 15:22 GNT

Write down the advice of him who loves you, though you like it not at present.

ENGLISH PROVERB

Say what?

Anyone who listens to correction is respected.

~ *Proverbs 13:18 GNT*

Michele believed her boss was critical and impossible to please. No matter what she did, according to Mr. Branigan, Michele could have and should have been doing it better: "Don't put so much salt on the fries." "Count back the change out loud to the customer." "Smile and make eye contact when you're taking an order."

Who does he think he is? I'm only serving fast food. What's the big deal about doing every little thing just right? When Mr. Branigan fired Michele after only three weeks on the job, she knew it had nothing to do with her. It was his bad attitude.

The one thing Michele didn't understand was how her friend Kelly could still work for Mr. Branigan—and like it. "I try my best to do things the way he shows me," Kelly told her. "I figure he's trying to help me do a better job." Michele hadn't considered that Mr. Branigan was trying to help her. She had thought he was just picking on her.

The way you receive criticism has more to do with attitude than the words being spoken. You may feel you're being criticized unfairly when someone is only trying to help you. Or you may be trying to ignore God's prompting in your life to change your ways. Hearing the truth may make you feel guilty—and defensive. Next time this happens to you, swallow your pride and listen. More times than not these suggestions will spur interpersonal growth and confidence.

Try this: Remember the notebook you started in "God's Gift to Parents"? It's time to add the criticism as well as the advice you receive—whether it comes from your parents, teachers, siblings, friends, or your boss. Do different pieces of advice or criticism say the same thing? Don't forget to review your notebook once a month and evaluate the insights that you gain.

HE WHO LISTENS TO A LIFE-GIVING REBUKE WILL BE AT HOME AMONG THE WISE.

PROVERBS 15:31 NIV

ANYTHING YOU SAY TO THE WISE WILL MAKE THEM WISER.

PROVERBS 9:9 GNT

The trouble with most of us is that we would rather be ruined by praise than saved by criticism.

NORMAN VINCENT PEALE

The Humble Heart

Doing your best without needing applause

Giving in secret to aid a good cause

Facing the truth when you make a mistake

Stepping aside for someone else's sake

Knowing your victories are God's work of art

These are the signs of a pure, humble heart.

Cathryn Atkinson

If you are humble, you will be respected.

— *Proverbs* 29:23 GNT

When pride comes, then comes disgrace; but wisdom is with the humble.

— *Proverbs* 11:2 NRSV

JUST AS DARKNESS RETREATS BEFORE LIGHT, SO ALL ANGER AND BITTERNESS DISAPPEAR BEFORE THE FRAGRANCE OF HUMILITY.

JOHN CLIMACUS

As If!

Charcoal keeps the embers glowing, wood keeps the fire burning, and troublemakers keep arguments alive.

~ *Proverbs 26:21* GNT

QUARRELS
WOULD NOT LAST
LONG IF THE
FAULT WERE ONLY
ON ONE SIDE.
—LA
ROCHEFOUCAULD

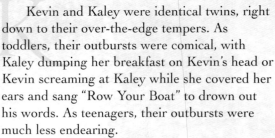

Kevin and Kaley were identical twins, right down to their over-the-edge tempers. As toddlers, their outbursts were comical, with Kaley dumping her breakfast on Kevin's head or Kevin screaming at Kaley while she covered her ears and sang "Row Your Boat" to drown out his words. As teenagers, their outbursts were much less endearing.

"He just knows what to say to tick me off," Kaley explained to her friend.

When Amber suggested that the next time Kevin tried to bait Kaley into an argument she should keep her mouth shut, Kaley couldn't believe what she was hearing. Why should she have to take it and not dish it back? Since when did she have to play the mature one? After all, Kevin was the older brother—by two minutes, anyway.

But it only took a minute for Kaley to reconsider Amber's suggestion. *She's right*, Kaley realized. *I'll just keep quiet. I won't let Kevin goad me into another argument.*

A fire cannot grow without a constant source of fuel. Responding in anger to someone who's giving you a hard time doesn't solve anything. It just makes everyone's anger burn a little hotter. God has given you the gift of self-control—the ability to be quiet. Whether you choose to use that gift when faced with an argument or use your words to throw fuel on the flames is completely up to you.

Try this: *The next time you see two people on TV get into an argument, figure out how they could have stopped it. What would have happened if one of the characters refused to continue the argument and spoke back to the other in love instead of anger? What did you learn that you can apply to your own life?*

A GENTLE ANSWER QUIETS ANGER, BUT A HARSH ONE STIRS IT UP.

PROVERBS 15:1 GNT

THE START OF AN ARGUMENT IS LIKE THE FIRST BREAK IN A DAM; STOP IT BEFORE IT GOES ANY FURTHER.

PROVERBS 17:14 GNT

Discussion is an exchange of knowledge; argument is an exchange of ignorance.

ROBERT QUILLEN

I'll Never Do That Again

If you are wise, you will learn when you are corrected.

~ *Proverbs* 19:25 GNT

If everybody makes mistakes, why does it seem like other people blow it in private, while you screw up right in front of the cutest guy or girl in school? Okay, so maybe it just feels that way. That's because making a mistake can make you feel like a total loser.

Doing something dumb isn't all bad. Making mistakes actually gives you a chance to do something smart by learning from them. That sounds like something your parents might say after you've backed your car into a fire hydrant during your driver's test, but it's true. Best of all, you can learn not only from your own mistakes, but from the mistakes of others. (Yes, they do make them—honest.)

The next time you, or a friend, do something like flunk a chemistry test by waiting until the last minute to memorize the periodic tables, take advantage of that mistake. Learn not to repeat it.

Mistakes teach two different kinds of lessons. The first is how to be humble. No one does everything perfectly, except God. When you make a mistake, or someone else does, it's time for forgiveness, acceptance, and encouragement. Don't put yourself or someone else down for doing something wrong. God doesn't. Second, learn what not to do in the future. If you see your friend do something that has a bad outcome, don't follow his or her example—learn from the mistake.

TRY THIS: *Play the "Top Ten Dumbest Things I've Ever Done" with your close Christian friends. Share the biggest mistakes you've ever made, even the embarrassing ones. Then share the lessons you learned from them. Be sure to laugh with each other, not at each other. You're bound to learn a little humility and some great things not to do as you seek to.*

IF YOU REFUSE TO LEARN, YOU ARE HURTING YOURSELF.

PROVERBS 15:32 GNT

INTELLIGENT PEOPLE WANT TO LEARN.

PROVERBS 15:14 GNT

Learn from the mistakes of others—you can't live long enough to make them all yourself.

MARTIN VANBEE

Getting It Done

Being lazy will make you poor, but hard work will make you rich.

— *Proverbs 10:4 GNT*

Summer break was finally here and Drew wasn't going to waste a minute of it. With his junior year behind him, all Drew wanted to do was spend time with friends, play disc golf, and eat junk food.

His mom talked to him about getting a job, but Drew had worked hard all year, and next summer he would be getting ready for college. He'd passed all of his classes—except pre-calc. *So what? I can repeat that in the fall. This is my last chance to have some fun.*

The first two weeks were great, but after that most of Drew's friends were busy with jobs of their own. When they did get together, Drew rarely had money to to the movies or help pay for gas. Soon his friends started grumbling about Drew always mooching off them. He had anticipated a carefree summer filled with fun. It seemed instead like he was experiencing just the opposite. Drew began to rethink his decision.

Maybe getting a job wouldn't be the end of the world, after all.

Every person has a special place in this world—and it isn't on the couch in front of the TV. Right now your place is to be a student, a friend, a member of a family and, perhaps, an employee. God said that whatever you do you should work at it with all your heart. That doesn't mean you never get time to relax. Even God took a day off after creating the world. It just means you should show up for life. That's what really makes life worth living.

Try this: Give up TV for a week. Use this time instead to write a letter to a friend, get some exercise, or give your room that long overdue cleaning. At the end of the week review everything you've done. How do you feel about what you've accomplished? Do you feel like you could give up TV for another week? Go ahead, it's okay.

A HARD WORKER WILL GET EVERYTHING HE WANTS.

PROVERBS 13:4 GNT

DILIGENT HANDS WILL RULE.

PROVERBS 12:24 NIV

Diligence is the mother of good fortune, and idleness, its opposite, never brought a man to the goal of any of his best wishes.

CERVANTES

Constant Companions

The righteous person is a guide to his friend.

~ *Proverbs 12:26* GNT

There was no way Mariah was going to let her mom pick her friends. Just because Rachel had been caught shoplifting and was suspended from school a couple of times didn't make her a "bad influence." Mariah knew what was right and wrong.

As they walked around the mall, Mariah was repeating her mom's latest lecture to Rachel. But the moment they left the department store, a security guard grabbed them by the arm. "What's your problem? We didn't do anything," Mariah said, her voice trembling.

That's when the guard pulled the pair of earrings out of Mariah's purse. Now she was really confused. As the guard walked the girls back to the office to call their parents and talk to the store manager, Rachel mouthed *I'm sorry* to Mariah. Rachel must have dropped the earrings in Mariah's purse while she was rambling on at the jewelry counter about her mom.

Mariah finally understood what her mom had been concerned about.

Sometimes nice people make poor choices or take foolish risks. You may be friends with them because you enjoy their company or maybe you just want to try to help them out. The problem is that it's easy to get pulled down. If a friend of yours is doing something that makes you uncomfortable, cool the relationship for a while and simply pray for that person. God knows exactly what your friend needs.

Try this: Think of a friend who's had a positive influence in your life. Honor that person by writing a letter, telling your friend why your life is better because he or she is part of it and how you would like to strive to attain their qualities. Deliver your letter in person, if possible; if not, make sure to send it.

He who walks with the wise grows wise.

Proverbs 13:20 NIV

Do not be fooled. Bad companions ruin good character.

I Corinthians 15:33 GNT

No one can be provident of his time who is not prudent in the choice of his company.

Jeremy Taylor

The Kind Heart

Do you wish the world were happy?
Then remember, day by day,
Just to scatter seeds of kindness
As you pass along the way;
For the pleasures of the many
May be oft times traced to one,
As the hand that plants the acorn
Shelters armies from the sun.

Author Unknown

Worry can rob you of happiness, but kind words will cheer you up.

— *Proverbs* 12:25 GNT

He who despises his neighbor sins, but blessed is he who is kind to the needy.

— *Proverbs* 14:21 NIV

KINDNESS IS A LANGUAGE THAT THE DUMB CAN SPEAK AND THE DEAF CAN HEAR.

AUTHOR UNKNOWN

Oops! I Did It Again

Enthusiasm without knowledge is not good; impatience will get you into trouble.

~ *Proverbs* 19:2 GNT

HE WHO
HESITATES IS
SOMETIMES
SAVED.
—JAMES THURBER

From where Grady was standing, it looked like he'd carved the Grand Canyon into the front end of his friend's car. At least the streetlight didn't seem worse for wear. *If only that cat hadn't run out in front of me,* Grady thought. *How could I be so careless. I'm going to be grounded for life—maybe worse.*

Grady didn't have his license yet. Actually, he hadn't even started driver's training. But he'd watched people drive for almost sixteen years. It didn't look hard.

What was really going to be difficult was explaining why the invitation to take his friend's new car out for a spin had actually sounded like a good idea just moments before.

Grady's parents had discussed getting him a car of his own this summer. *This is going to change everything,* Grady thought, wishing he could erase the last five minutes and start over again.

⁂ Time only goes one way—forward. The choices you make today may have consequences you'll be living with tomorrow, the next day, and even the rest of your life. That's why emotions or peer pressure shouldn't drive decisions. When you feel yourself being pushed to make a decision, listen to your instincts (the inner wisdom you've accumulated) and don't act hastily. Take time to think through your decisions.

⁂ TRY THIS: *Practice saying "Let me think about it—I'll let you know" while facing yourself in the mirror. Keep practicing until you achieve an acceptable level of confidence. Then, the next time you feel the pressure to make a quick decision, whether it's joining your friends for a party or responding to a salesperson at the mall, repeat those words. This will allow you the time to make a good decision.*

BE WISE AND GIVE
SERIOUS THOUGHT
TO THE WAY
YOU LIVE.

PROVERBS 23:19 GNT

THIS IS WHAT THE
LORD ALMIGHTY
SAYS, "GIVE
CAREFUL THOUGHT
TO YOUR WAYS."

HAGGAI 1:7 NIV

There is a time when we must firmly choose the course we will follow, or the relentless drift of events will make the decision.

HERBERT V. PROCHNOW

Where's the Manual?

If you listen to advice and are willing to learn, one day you will be wise.

— *Proverbs* 19:20 GNT

BLESSED ARE
THOSE WHO
LISTEN, FOR THEY
SHALL LEARN.
—AUTHOR
UNKNOWN

Picture this—it's the morning of your birthday and there's a big box sitting on the kitchen table. You bypass the homemade waffles and head straight for the package. After some frantic unwrapping, you discover your folks have bought you a new computer. Unfortunately, there's one thing missing—the owner's manual. Now, unless you totally understand computers, the fun comes to a screeching halt. There's no way you can get your computer up and running, let alone master everything it can do, without a little help.

Life works the same way. It's so complex that it's impossible to figure it out on your own. Luckily, there are walking, talking, breathing, loving instruction manuals all around you. The advice and example of parents, teachers, and mentors can be a priceless resource, especially during your teen years. The choice is up to you. An instruction manual is useless, unless you choose to follow what's written inside.

A student can have an excellent teacher and still flunk a class. Why? Because learning is a choice. Choosing to listen, remember something, and then act on what you've learned takes effort on your part, and it takes a teachable heart. Begin by recognizing you don't know it all. Be open to learn something new—from the lesson, from the school, and from God. Be prepared to learn, and then put what you've learned into practice. That turns a smart person into a wise one.

Try this: Select a mentor. This may be a teacher or counselor at school, a church youth leader, or another significant adult in your life. Your mentor needs to be someone you trust and respect. Get together at least once a month to talk over big decisions and big questions about life. Get ready to listen and learn.

FOLLOW THE WAY OF KNOWLEDGE.

PROVERBS 9:6 GNT

JESUS SAID, "WHATEVER YOU HAVE LEARNED OR RECEIVED OR HEARD FROM ME, OR SEEN IN ME—PUT IT INTO PRACTICE. AND THE GOD OF PEACE WILL BE WITH YOU."

PHILIPPIANS 4:9 NIV

As long as you live, keep learning how to live.

SENECA

Teamwork

Anxiety weighs down the human heart, but a good word cheers it up.

— *Proverbs 12:25 NRSV*

Kevin noticed that Greg seemed to be in a perpetual bad mood—except when he was playing basketball. Whether he was enduring a grueling practice or playing at the state playoffs, once Greg had the ball in his hands, he almost seemed to dance down the court. But Greg's smile ended with the sound of the final buzzer. In the locker room, he quickly returned to his sullen self.

"What's up with him?" Colin asked Kevin after a particularly sweet victory—and a temperamental hasty retreat by Greg.

Kevin had been Greg's friend since kindergarten, and he'd never known him to be so moody. Only a couple of months ago Greg had been joking and fooling around with his buddies after games. *Maybe he's got a problem I don't know about.*

"Beats me." Kevin said to Colin. Then he added, "Why don't we try and catch up with him? Maybe sharing a pizza might loosen him up—it couldn't hurt to ask."

Anxiety isn't always easy to spot. It can come across as anger, depression or apathy. It may even manifest itself as an eating disorder, a willingness to take unnecessary risks, or a pattern of getting involved in unhealthy relationships. Be sensitive to those around you. When you see someone who seems to be struggling with anxiety, don't just walk away and pretend that it's someone else's problem. Risk reaching out. Pray for that person regularly. And ask God what you can do to help.

Try this: Share a good word with someone today. Write a letter, make a phone call, or just ask that person face-to-face, "How are you doing — really?" It could be a friend who's going through a hard time or just a person who's been on your mind. You never know. You may just be the high point in that person's day.

Anxiety does not empty tomorrow of its sorrows, but only empties today of its strength.

C. H. SPURGEON

I Want That

The greedy person stirs up strife, but whoever trusts in the LORD will be enriched.

— Proverbs 28:25 NRSV

Amber had a hard time listening to her friend Gwen these last few days. Ever since her birthday, all Gwen did was complain about her parents not buying her the new snowboard she wanted. Amber tried to point out that Gwen had received a perfectly good used board. But they'd been friends long enough for Amber to know that Gwen felt that she had to own whatever was the latest, hottest, most expensive thing at the mall. A used board would never do.

Amber had to admit, the board Gwen had picked out was awesome. It easily cost four times what the used board had cost. But the used board was a classic in terrific shape. Amber would have loved to have had it.

Amber still had to rent all of her equipment. Not only that, she had to pay for it with her own money. *I wonder why Gwen can't just enjoy what she has instead of always trying to get what she doesn't have?*

Greed is a kind of hunger. It's a craving to possess something that will make you feel better on the inside or look better on the outside. It's an attempt to fill up your heart—with things. The problem is, the more you feed greed, the hungrier it grows. The only thing that leaves a heart feeling fully satisfied is a relationship with God. God's love doesn't just fill your heart, it makes it bigger, changing your focus from "what can I get" to "what can I give."

Try this: Instead of buying something this week, give some time away. Donate your service to a charity; mow the neighbor's lawn and refuse payment; bake cookies for the next church fellowship; or give your time to a nonprofit organization. Record your gifts of time in your journal, and thank God for the abilities and blessings he has given you.

HE THAT IS GREEDY OF GAIN TROUBLETH HIS OWN HOUSE; BUT HE THAT HATETH GIFTS SHALL LIVE.

PROVERBS 15:27 KJV

JESUS SAID, "WATCH OUT! BE ON YOUR GUARD AGAINST ALL KINDS OF GREED; A MAN'S LIFE DOES NOT CONSIST IN THE ABUNDANCE OF HIS POSSESSIONS."

LUKE 12:15 NIV

There is enough in the world for everyone's need, but not enough for everyone's greed.

FRANK BUCHMAN

The Faithful Heart

Where the going's smooth and pleasant

You will always find the throng,

For the many—more's the pity—

Seem to like to drift along.

But the steps that call for courage

And the task that's hard to do

In the end results in glory

For the never wavering few!

Author Unknown

48

Never let go of loyalty and faithfulness. Tie them around your neck; write them on your heart.

~ *Proverbs 3:3* GNT

He that is faithful in that which is least is faithful also in much.

~ *Luke 16:10* KJV

FAITHFULNESS AND TRUTH ARE THE MOST SACRED EXCELLENCES AND ENDOWMENTS OF THE HUMAN MIND.

CICERO

What's In It for Me?

People who do not get along with others are interested only in themselves.

— *Proverbs* 18:1 GNT

"No way," Jeff told Ben angrily. "You lost your putting disc. That's your problem." Ben walked out of the room without a word. He knew it was no use arguing with his older brother. Jeff couldn't even believe Ben had the nerve to ask to borrow his stuff. After all, Jeff had paid for those discs with his own money.

Of course, Ben's too young to get a job of his own, Jeff thought. And losing discs happens all the time on the course. Jeff had lost one disc golfing just a couple of weeks ago. Luckily, he had the money to replace it.

Jeff felt a twinge of remorse. Maybe he'd been too hard on Ben. Lending his younger brother a disc probably wouldn't cost him anything more than a little aggravation. Jeff picked up his yellow putter and headed for Ben's room.

Selfishness means to be overly concerned with your own personal interest. It's pretty easy to see in others, but not so easy to see in yourself. Sometimes it's tough to decide if you're being selfish or just taking care of your things. God can help you see the difference. When someone asks to borrow one of your possessions, and you find yourself hesitating, ask yourself why you don't want to share. You may find your answer says more about you than it does about the other person.

TRY THIS: *Spend a few moments rewriting your life. Change the place where you were born to a country where most people live in poor circumstances. What do you think your past, present, and future might look like? Thank God for what he's given you and ask how you can better share what you've received with others.*

A GENEROUS MAN WILL PROSPER; HE WHO REFRESHES OTHERS WILL HIMSELF BE REFRESHED.

PROVERBS 11:25 NIV

DO NOT SEEK YOUR OWN ADVANTAGE, BUT THAT OF THE OTHER.

I CORINTHIANS 10:24 NRSV

The least-used words by an unselfish person are, I, me, my, and mine.

CHARLES R. SWINDOLL

That's Just Dumb

Good sense wins favor, but the way of the faithless is their ruin.
~ *Proverbs* 13:15 NRSV

Products often come with warning labels on them to protect a manufacturer from being sued if a product is used incorrectly. Sometimes, though, it seems that the manufacturer goes a bit too far in trying to protect the consumer. Consider these actual warnings found on products:

On child's stroller: Remove child before folding.

On hose nozzle: Do not spray into electrical outlet.

On box of nails: WARNING—Do not swallow nails. May cause irritation.

On blow dryer: Do not blow-dry hair in sleep.

On child's superhero costume: CAUTION— Cape does not enable user to fly.

Why would labels like these be necessary? For the majority of consumers, they're not. Warnings like these are written solely for people who may lack good sense. A lack of good sense may lead you to do something downright dangerous. That's why developing good sense makes perfect sense.

52

Some people act like good sense is difficult to come by. But that just isn't so. The Bible, particularly the book of Proverbs, is full of sound advice on how to develop good sense. Other great resources are parents, grandparents, and teachers. Good sense can by obtained by watching the lives of those around you and learning from their successes and failures. Don't settle for less. Learn to access the sources of good sense in your life until you're able to follow them straight to the top.

TRY THIS: *Come up with three warning labels to help you develop good sense in your own life. Put them where you'll see them, like on the bathroom mirror or in your school locker. For instance, you could put one on the notebook of advice you're creating that says "WARNING: Not following good advice may mean making the same mistake twice."*

SENSIBLE PEOPLE ACCEPT GOOD ADVICE.

PROVERBS 10:8 GNT

SENSIBLE PEOPLE WILL SEE TROUBLE COMING AND AVOID IT.

PROVERBS 22:3 GNT

Wisdom is an affair of values and value judgments. It is intelligent conduct of human affairs.

SIDNEY HOOK

Lean on Me

Like a bad tooth or a lame foot is trust in a faithless person in time of trouble.

— *Proverbs 25:19 NRSV*

FAITHFULNESS IN
LITTLE THINGS IS
A BIG THING.
—SAINT JOHN
CHRYSOSTOM

Sarah glanced at her watch one more time. The movie was going to start any minute, but Felicity's blue pickup truck was still nowhere to be seen. Sarah wondered why she'd ever asked Felicity for a ride in the first place. She knew how unreliable Felicity was sometimes. But Felicity was her best friend, and that had to count for something.

Sarah sighed and gave Felicity's cell phone one more ring. No answer. *She probably just forgot to turn it on — as usual*, Sarah thought. So much for meeting the rest of the volleyball team at the theater.

As Felicity's truck roared around the corner, Sarah decided the movie could wait until another time. Instead, she'd ask Felicity if they could just talk. *Maybe what she really needs to hear from me*, Sarah thought, *is that being a real friend means being someone others can count on.*

Promises don't only happen if you cross your heart. Every time you say you're going to do something, you're really saying "I promise." Following through on these everyday promises is how you become dependable. It's how you earn the trust of those around you. This means doing what you say you'll do, even if it ends up being inconvenient or you have to turn down a better offer. It means keeping your word. It means being a friend in the truest sense of the word.

Try this: Think back over the last month. Are there any promises you've made that you haven't yet fulfilled? Maybe you told your mom you'd clean the bathroom, but you haven't followed through. Or maybe you promised to give the new kid at school a call sometime and haven't gotten around to it. Don't wait any longer. Make a list and stand by your word.

Don't let love and truth ever leave you.

Proverbs 3:3 NIRV

Do as you promised, so that your name will be great forever.

2 Samuel 7:25–26 NIV

God did not call us to be successful, but to be faithful.

Mother Teresa

Money, Money, Money

Those who depend on their wealth will fall like the leaves of autumn, but the righteous will prosper like the leaves of summer.

— *Proverbs* 11:28 GNT

MONEY HAS
NEVER YET MADE
ANYONE RICH.
—SENECA

He'd flipped burgers, washed cars, and even walked dogs. Gary had worked all summer so he'd have enough money to buy a car in the fall. "Sure you don't want to join us?" his friends would ask whenever they headed off to the beach. "It's your last summer of freedom."

What Gary looked forward to, however, was the freedom he'd have his senior year with a car of his own. But that was before his dad got laid off. Gary knew how the bills were piling up.

He put down the automotive section of the classifieds and borrowed his parents' van. Once he arrived at Central Trust Bank, he took the money out of his savings account and slipped it into his dad's birthday card. He wasn't even sure his dad would accept it. But Gary was sure of one thing—it was the right thing to do.

Money is nothing more than a tool. How well you use it is really where its value is found. Although many people find security in the size of their bank account, money isn't the answer to every problem. Only God can make that claim. Managing your money wisely is one way of thanking God for what he's given you. Making wise financial decisions allows you to better take care of your needs, handle the unexpected, and help others less fortunate than yourself.

TRY THIS: *A good rule for being wise with your money is to save ten percent, give away or tithe ten percent, invest ten percent, and live off the rest. Saving, spending, and investing are self-explanatory, but the ten percent you give away, according to God's principles, should go to him. This can be given to your church, where it can be used to help others in need. Why not start today?*

DO NOT WEAR YOURSELF OUT TO GET RICH.

PROVERBS 23:4 NIV

YOUR HEART WILL ALWAYS BE WHERE YOUR RICHES ARE.

LUKE 12:34 GNT

If a person gets his attitude toward money straight, it will help straighten out almost every other area in his life.

BILLY GRAHAM

The Loving Heart

I love you,

Not only for what you are,

But for what I am

When I am with you.

I love you,

Not only for what

You have made of yourself,

But for what you are making of me.

Author Unknown

Anyone who wants to be godly and loving finds life, success and honor.

— *Proverbs 21:21 NIRV*

If we love one another, God lives in us, and his love is perfected in us.

—*1 John 4:12 NRSV*

HE WHO LOVES HIS
FELLOW MAN IS
LOVING GOD THE
BEST HE CAN.

ALICE CARY

All the Wrong Moves

Sensible people are careful to stay out of trouble.

~ *Proverbs 14:16* GNT

God does not
care what
good you did
but why you
did it.
—Angelus
Silesius

When Karen saw the police officer's flashlight through the car window, she felt scared and relieved at the same time. She never meant to end up parked on a dark road with her new boyfriend. *After tonight, ex-boyfriend will be more accurate,* she thought.

Everyone at school knew about Carl's reputation, including Karen. But she had been so flattered when he asked her out that she couldn't think of anything else to say, but yes. How could she have been this naive? It didn't take long to realize that Carl was more concerned with making his old girlfriend jealous than with getting to know Karen.

Karen had hoped tonight would be different. Carl had offered to take her for a romantic drive. When he didn't say one word to her all the way to Taylor Park, Karen should've known something was wrong. Now all Karen could think was *Why didn't I listen to my head instead of my heart?*

What does a caution sign mean? Slow down and proceed with care—potential danger ahead. That's helpful on the road, but wouldn't it be great if there was a caution sign that would appear before you made a bad decision? Actually, that equipment comes standard in most humans. It's called your conscience. God designed your conscience to slow you down enough to evaluate facts and learn from mistakes, then choose to avoid danger. Whether you choose to pay attention to God's caution sign or not is up to you.

Try this: Make or buy a CAUTION road sign to hang in your room or on your bathroom mirror. Every morning, use it as a visual reminder to slow down and proceed with caution as you make choices throughout the day. Gather the facts, weigh the consequences, and don't forget to pay attention when that signs appears.

PRESERVE SOUND JUDGMENT AND DISCERNMENT, DO NOT LET THEM OUT OF YOUR SIGHT. . . . THEN YOU WILL GO ON YOUR WAY IN SAFETY, AND YOUR FOOT WILL NOT STUMBLE.

PROVERBS 3:21, 23
NIV

THORNS AND SNARES ARE IN THE WAY OF THE PERVERSE; THE CAUTIOUS WILL KEEP FAR FROM THEM.

PROVERBS 22:5
NRSV

Some persons do first, think afterward, and then repent forever.

THOMAS SECKER

61

What's in a Name?

A good name is more desirable than great riches.
— *Proverbs 22:1 NIV*

What kind of person comes to mind when you think of each of these words: *dictator, peacemaker, tyrant, martyr, miser, savior*? The picture that comes to mind changes with every word, doesn't it? Real life individuals who live up to one of these titles have been labeled according to what they've done, judged according to their reputation. Fair or not, people will do the same thing to you every day of your life. Their picture of who you are will be built on the reputation you've earned.

The funny thing is, it's easier to earn a reputation as a jerk than as a saint. Flunk a class, you might be labeled stupid. Get a new car, you might be labeled spoiled. Have lots of guy friends, you could be labeled easy. To be labeled loving, generous, patient, hardworking, or trustworthy takes time. These characteristics have to consistently be seen in your life to earn a reputation that's as good as gold.

Suppose you were being introduced to a group of people at a party, when someone came up to you and said, "Oh, I've heard about you." What would you think they'd heard? The reputation you're building today is the one you'll have to work with as an adult, for better or for worse. If your life centers on God's wisdom, not just on your own, chances are that your reputation will be a good one, both in heaven and here on earth.

Try this: If possible, find out what your name means. One way is to search the Internet under "baby names." Or you could ask your parents what the name means to them and why they chose it. Then evaluate how your life is measuring up to the positive qualities your name points out. Is there any character quality in your name that you'd be proud to live up to?

THE MEMORY OF THE RIGHTEOUS WILL BE A BLESSING.

PROVERBS 10:7 NIV

A GOOD NAME IS BETTER THAN FINE PERFUME.

ECCLESIASTES 7:1 NIV

Glass, china, and reputation are easily crack'd and never well mended.

BENJAMIN FRANKLIN

SOMETHING THAT COUNTS

If your goals are good, you will be respected, but if you are looking for trouble, that is what you will get.

~ *Proverbs* 11:27 GNT

As Ron headed down the street toward home, Nathan waved after him from the front porch. Then he turned his attention to Derek, who was standing behind him "You hanging out with junior high kids now, Nathan?" Derek asked with a smirk.

When Nathan explained to Derek that he tutored Ron in math every other Monday afternoon, Derek thought it sounded like a good way to make a few extra bucks. But when Nathan further explained that he was doing it for free, Derek smiled and shook his head. "Whatever," Derek responded.

"Hey, I like doing it," said Nathan. "Math is easy for me and hard for Ron. Helping him just seems like a good thing to do. Most afternoons I just kind of hang out anyway. Haven't you ever done something just because it makes you feel good inside?"

Everyone's heard the expression "looking for trouble," but have you ever heard of someone being accused of "looking for good?" Chances are, if you're looking for something diligently enough, eventually you'll find it. So why not search for something good, something positive to put your time, talents, and energy toward? You'll soon discover that doing good feels good. Better yet, it allows you to make a positive difference in the world. No act of kindness is too small to make an impact.

TRY THIS: *Today, look for good. Keep your eyes and heart open. Look for opportunities to do something positive—no matter how small. It may be just holding a door for someone or picking up your dinner dishes without being asked. It may be noticing the trash and taking it out before being asked. How many opportunities can you find?*

WHENEVER YOU POSSIBLY CAN, DO GOOD TO THOSE WHO NEED IT.

PROVERBS 3:27 GNT

AS OFTEN AS WE HAVE THE CHANCE, WE SHOULD DO GOOD TO EVERYONE.

GALATIANS 6:10 GNT

Measure your day, not by what you harvest, but by what you plant.

AUTHOR UNKNOWN

What to Do?

Do what is right and fair; that pleases the LORD more than bringing him sacrifices.

~ Proverbs 21:3 GNT

Suppose you saw a bag fall out of the back door of a truck. Then, suppose that when you picked up the bag you discovered that it was filled with money, lots of money—$120,000. And suppose that at the time you were a single mother of five children, with lots of overdue bills, working at a job that only paid $7.88 an hour. What would you do?

According to a story in *People Weekly*, that actually happened to a woman named Wanda Johnson. Do you think that Wanda considered this windfall as God's providence and tucked it away for her children's food, clothing, shelter, medical needs, and education?

But that's not what Wanda did. She spent some time praying, and then called the police so that the money could be returned to the company that the money belonged to. Wanda did receive a cash reward for returning the bag, but she didn't know that was going to happen. All she knew was that she had to do the right thing.

Doing the right thing isn't always easy, but it's still always the right thing to do. You may convince yourself that doing the wrong thing wouldn't hurt anyone, that no would ever know. You'd be wrong on both counts. Choosing to do something you know is wrong hurts your character and the God who loves you. God knows everything you do, even in secret. Doing what's right is a gift to him. It also affords you a guilt-free conscience and joy in knowing your heavenly Father is proud of you.

Try this: Watch the evening news or read today's paper. Choose one story from the headlines where someone chose to do the wrong thing. Make a list of all the bad things that happened as a result of this one wrong act. Then make a list of the positive things that could have happened if this person had done the right thing. Evaluate the consequences of bad choices.

No matter how often honest people fall, they always get up again.

Proverbs 24:16 GNT

Honest people will lead a full, happy life.

Proverbs 28:20 GNT

Better, though difficult, the right way to go than wrong, tho' easy, where the end is woe.

John Bunyan

The Gentle Heart

Gentle on the wings of whispers
Tender in the arms of night
Softly now his steps surround me
In the early morning light.
Words of healing now he offers,
"My child, give all your hurts to me."
Quietly my burdens lifting
Gentle Savior, lost in Thee.

Andrea Garney

*A gentle answer
quiets anger.*

— *Proverbs* 15:1 GNT

*Let your gentleness be
evident to all.*

— *Philippians* 4:5 NIV

Nothing is so
strong as
gentleness,
nothing so
gentle as real
strength.

Saint Francis de Sales

APPLY A LITTLE PRAYER

Do not rejoice when your enemies fall, and do not let your heart be glad when they stumble.

— Proverbs 24:17 NRSV

THE BEST WAY
TO DESTROY AN
ENEMY IS TO
MAKE HIM A
FRIEND.
—ABRAHAM
LINCOLN

Stacy and Melissa were friends. But when Melissa made the cheerleading team and Stacy didn't, everything changed. Stacy wouldn't even speak to Melissa when they passed in the hall, and Melissa soon heard that Stacy was saying unkind things about her to classmates. She felt hurt and angered by Stacy's actions. *I'm sorry Stacy didn't make the team, but why is she blaming me?* Melissa thought.

Then a few days later, Melissa overheard two girls talking, "Hey, did you hear that Stacy didn't make the soccer team or the track team?" one told the other. "When it comes to sports, Stacy should just sit in the stands."

Melissa felt a wave of satisfaction. Stacy was getting what she deserved. Then, just as quickly, she felt a surge of conscience. She remembered that the Bible says not to rejoice when one's enemy stumbles. *I should pray for her,* Melissa thought.

You may have felt that little nudge of satisfaction when you heard that one of your adversaries got what was coming to him or her. After all, that person deserved it, right? It seems right, but God has a better idea. He says that you should not rejoice when your enemy stumbles. Instead, you should pray for him or her. That doesn't mean you necessarily need to be friends—wisdom should guide you. Ask God to show you how to please him in the situation.

TRY THIS: *If you find that you have an adversary, write his or her name on a small card and date it. Don't write anything about that person being an enemy, just the name and date. Keep the card out of sight by your bed. Each night, take out the card, pray that God will bless and care for that person, then put the date on the back. See how long it takes for God to change your heart.*

WHEN YOU PLEASE THE LORD, YOU CAN MAKE YOUR ENEMIES INTO FRIENDS.

PROVERBS 16:7 GNT

JESUS SAID, "LOVE YOUR ENEMIES AND DO GOOD TO THOSE WHO HATE YOU."

LUKE 6:27 GNT

Do good to your friend to keep him, to your enemy to gain him.

BENJAMIN FRANKLIN

The Truth About Lies

One who gives an honest answer gives a kiss on the lips.

~ *Proverbs 24:26 NRSV*

Taylor didn't consider himself a liar. After all, he assured himself, everybody tells little lies when he's in a tight spot. And the spot Taylor found himself in right now would certainly qualify. His older brother Kevin's new acoustic guitar had a big scratch across the front of it — thanks to Taylor.

All Taylor wanted to do was try it out. He knew he wasn't supposed to be in his brother's room, let alone touch his prized possession. Taylor intended to be very careful. At least that had been the plan until a little high-spirited jamming ended in a collision with the bedpost.

When Kevin got home and saw his marred guitar, he was really angry. He stormed into Taylor's room, demanding an explanation. "Hey, I didn't do it," Taylor said. Now Taylor was accusing Sam, their younger brother. *Better him than me*, Taylor thought to himself, but he knew what he'd done was wrong. Taylor headed down the hall to tell Kevin the truth.

72

Not every lie is a whopper. But every lie, no matter how small, has consequences. If what you say is false, you're setting yourself up to be a person whose word can't be trusted. Or you may find yourself trying to live with the fact that someone else took the blame for something you did. That can lead to broken relationships and a damaged reputation. Even if your lies are believed, you're stuck living with them. Ask God to help you become a person who loves, values and practices the truth.

TRY THIS: *Try going through one whole day without exaggerating or telling a half-truth about something you've done, or without allowing someone else to take the blame for your actions. Strive to tell the whole truth. At the end of the day, write about the insights you've had regarding truth-telling and lying.*

DO NOT DECEIVE WITH YOUR LIPS.

PROVERBS 24:28
NRSV

WHEN YOU TELL THE TRUTH, JUSTICE IS DONE, BUT LIES LEAD TO INJUSTICE.

PROVERBS 12:17 GNT

A lie is a snowball: the further you roll it, the bigger it becomes.

MARTIN LUTHER

Doing It His Way

The human mind plans the way, but the LORD directs the steps.
— *Proverbs 16:9* NRSV

Sarah felt torn. She had been invited to spend spring break skiing in the mountains with her friend Nancy's family. Soon after she received the invitation, however, her church asked for volunteers to go on a trip to New Mexico, where they would help a small congregation finish their church building. Sarah really wanted to kick back and relax over spring break. But on Sunday, she felt God tugging at her heart as she looked around at the beautiful church building where she and her family worshiped.

Sarah talked to her parents about her dilemma and then to her friend. Nancy seemed disappointed at first. As Sarah explained what she had decided to do, Nancy's mood began to change.

"Hey, would your parents let you come along with me to New Mexico?" Sarah asked. A week later, the two friends were carrying their bags onto the church bus. The two friends agreed, it was a vacation they would never forget.

It's true. God's plans for you can be very different from your own, but his plans have a real advantage—a lasting sense of purpose and satisfaction. His plans will never disappoint. How will you know what his plans are? If you're listening with your heart and your eyes are open to the world around you, you'll know. You'll feel a stirring inside when you learn of a certain need or an unusual opportunity will come your way. You'll know it when you see it. He'll see to that.

TRY THIS: *Choose three adults in your life (for example, a parent, a teacher, your pastor, a grandparent, or a close friend of the family) to describe at least one situation where they put their own plans aside and did what they felt God was urging them to do. Listen carefully. Later, think about what you learned from their experiences.*

PEOPLE MAY PLAN ALL KINDS OF THINGS, BUT THE LORD'S WILL IS GOING TO BE DONE.

PROVERBS 19:21 GNT

"I KNOW THE PLANS I HAVE FOR YOU," DECLARES THE LORD, "PLANS TO PROSPER YOU AND NOT TO HARM YOU, PLANS TO GIVE YOU HOPE AND A FUTURE."

JEREMIAH 29:11 NIV

Inside the will of God there is no failure.

BERNARD EDINGER

Don't Tell Anyone, But . . .

Without wood, a fire goes out; without gossip, quarreling stops.

~ *Proverbs 26:20* GNT

THOSE WHO TALK ABOUT OTHERS TO US WILL TALK ABOUT US TO OTHERS.
—AUTHOR UNKNOWN

Have you ever noticed all those magazines along the checkout aisles in the grocery story? When the line is long, do you find yourself picking one up and looking for the latest information about your favorite celebrity? People are hungry to know every detail of celebrities' lives—whom they're dating, whom they've dumped, what they like on their pizza. That hunger for details is more than just casual interest. It's the seduction of gossip.

It's not just those in the public eye who end up being gossiped about. Often, it's people you know—friends, coworkers, classmates, teachers, even family members. Nearly everyone can be hurt by gossip—even you.

Like a forest fire, all it takes is one spark of gossip to start a four-alarm rumor. So be careful what you say and be careful what you listen to. Gossip can't start a fire if no one provides it with fuel. Don't be a person who passes along gossip. Be the kind of person who snuffs it out or simply passes it by.

Gossip isn't just a harmless pastime. It's a bittersweet addiction. It feels good to be "in the know," to be the center of attention because you have a story that will make your friends' hair curl. But gossip is not harmless. It can destroy relationships, hurt feelings, damage reputations, and do much more. How much better to be the voice of good news—kind, encouraging words that build up rather than tear down. Let your lips speak of things that bring life and love and loyalty. That's called fighting fire with fire.

No one who gossips can be trusted with a secret.

PROVERBS 11:13 GNT

Try this: The next time you find yourself in a conversation that's edging toward gossip, try to steer it in a different direction. Pass along a kindness that someone has done. Compliment someone. Mention something that builds up another person's reputation. Sing someone's praises. Notice how those around you respond.

A whisperer separates close friends.

PROVERBS 16:28 NRSV

The three essential rules when speaking of others are: Is it true? Is it kind? Is it necessary?

AUTHOR UNKNOWN

The Good Heart

Do all the good you can,

By all the means you can,

In all the ways you can,

In all the places you can,

At all the times you can,

To all the people you can,

As long as ever you can.

John Wesley

*When good people
pray, the LORD answers.*
— *Proverbs 15:29 GNT*

*Good people will be
rewarded for their deeds.*
— *Proverbs 14:14 GNT*

GOODNESS IS THE
ONLY INVESTMENT
THAT NEVER FAILS.

HENRY DAVID THOREAU

Bring It On

Pay attention to your teacher and learn all you can.

~ *Proverbs 23:12 GNT*

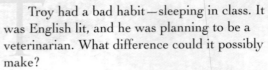

THEY KNOW
ENOUGH WHO
KNOW HOW
TO LEARN.
—HENRY ADAMS

Troy had a bad habit—sleeping in class. It was English lit, and he was planning to be a veterinarian. What difference could it possibly make?

Troy's English teacher explained to him that learning is about more than training for a profession. It's about becoming a well-rounded person who can move about in the world with ease. It's about creating a habit of learning that would help him for a lifetime. Troy was sleeping away his opportunities.

His teacher emphasized that English literature is more than words. Before long, Troy was learning new things in class—things like how to navigate relationships, how society and government work, the motivation behind world events, and the mystery of distant cultures. Before long, Troy found himself intrigued by what those poets, playwrights, and writers had to say. Troy understood that this was information that would guide him through his entire life.

The Bible says that God wants you to do all the learning you can. He wants you to learn about the world he created and learn how you are to function in it. He wants you to learn about yourself and those around you. He wants you to learn about him and what he has planned for your life. Learning isn't always easy and it isn't always fun, but it's always worthwhile. Books, teachers, and experiences are but a few of the many sources of learning. Honor God by determining to learn all you can.

TRY THIS: *Write your favorite teacher a thank-you note explaining how he or she has had a positive impact on your life. You may even want to throw in an apple for good measure. Believe it or not, teaching is just as much work as learning. Your note is guaranteed to make a teacher's day.*

THE WISE LAY UP KNOWLEDGE.

PROVERBS 10:14
NRSV

LET THE WISE LISTEN AND ADD TO THEIR LEARNING, AND LET THE DISCERNING GET GUIDANCE.

PROVERBS 1:5 NIV

Learning is not attained by chance. It must be sought for with ardor and attended to with diligence.

ABIGAIL ADAMS

Just One Little Drink

Drinking too much makes you loud and foolish.

~ *Proverbs 20:1* GNT

You've probably read or heard the statistics. Alcohol is the number one drug problem among teens. You probably know teens who drink, or maybe you have tried alcohol yourself. Teens who've tried alcohol are fifty percent more likely to try cocaine than teens who do not drink. Alcohol poisoning resulting in death is more prevalent in those under age twenty-five. Teenage girls are four times more likely to suffer from depression if they drink, while teenage guys decrease their chances of later fathering a child. Forty percent of kids who start drinking before the age of fifteen will become alcoholics later in life. Drinking can lead to vitamin deficiencies, stomach problems, liver damage, heart problems, kidney damage, memory loss, and even death.

The statistics start to hit home when you consider that every twenty-four hours, 11 teenagers will be killed and 350 injured, many permanently, in alcohol-related accidents. God loves you so much that he took the time to warn you about its dangers.

With everything you've learned so far about making wise decisions and developing good sense, it is pretty hard to think of drinking alcohol as anything but a foolish move. Not to mention that for teens, it's also illegal. Even if you believe you'll never become a statistic, the fact remains alcohol is expensive, it's a depressant, and it's addicting. It can ruin your looks, give you bad breath, make you gain weight, and mess with your muscles, your mind, your mouth—and your life. The disadvantages and dangers outweigh any perceived benefits, no matter how you look at it.

TRY THIS: *Make a list of things you can say if someone asks if you'd like an alcoholic beverage. They can be anything from "No, I'm not thirsty" to "I'd really just like a soft drink" to "I'm out of here." A good straightforward "no" also works wonders. How creative can you get?*

DON'T ASSOCIATE WITH PEOPLE WHO DRINK TOO MUCH WINE.

PROVERBS 23:20 GNT

DO NOT GET DRUNK WITH WINE, WHICH WILL ONLY RUIN YOU; INSTEAD BE FILLED WITH THE SPIRIT.

EPHESIANS 5:18 GNT

Alcohol does not drown care, but waters it and makes it grow faster.

BENJAMIN FRANKLIN

Walk on By

When sinners tempt you, don't give in.

~ Proverbs 1:10 GNT

Temptation is not a sin; it is a call to battle.
—Edwin W. Lutzer

In the television ads they'd seen, the movie seemed like silly, harmless fun. Stephanie and her friends had bowed to temptation and agreed to go in, even though it was rated R. But now Stephanie found herself blushing a lot more than laughing, and she could sense Karen's and Angie's discomfort in their seats on either side of her.

Maybe it'll get better, Stephanie thought. But a minute later, it got even worse. Stephanie pictured her parents sitting next to her and knew what they'd think. She took a deep breath, and then whispered to her friends, "I'm really not enjoying this. I'll wait for you guys out in the lobby."

When Stephanie reached the lobby, she was relieved to see Karen and Angie were right behind her.

"Wow. That was a pretty bad idea. What made us fall for those stupid ads?" she said.

"They were just a trick to make us buy a ticket."

What makes a temptation different from a regular, everyday desire? A temptation is the urge to do something you know is wrong. Temptations promise a chance at pleasure or personal gain. But temptations don't deliver on that promise. They leave you feeling guilty and conned. They can even be dangerous to your health and relationships—including your relationship with God. God promises that when you're tempted, he'll provide an escape. Choose to use it. Just walk away. You won't be missing a thing.

Sin leads only to more sin.

Proverbs 10:16 GNT

Try this: Everyone is tempted in different ways. What temptations have the greatest pull on your heart? Make a list of those things you'd be tempted to try, but that you know are wrong. Once you know where your weaknesses lie, you can choose to avoid situations where you'll find yourself face-to-face with those temptations.

God is faithful; he will not let you be tempted beyond what you can bear.

1 Corinthians 10:13 NIV

The devil tempts that he may ruin; God tests that he may crown.

Saint Ambrose

Because I Said So

Pay attention to what your father and mother tell you. Their teaching will improve your character.

~ *Proverbs 1:8–9 GNT*

OBEDIENCE IS
THE KEY TO
EVERY DOOR.
—GEORGE
MACDONALD

"Don't get on the Internet tonight. I'm expecting an important business call," Carlos's mom told him as she left for dinner with his dad. "Let the machine pick it up."

Carlos didn't give his mom's words another thought until he was finished with homework and there was nothing interesting on TV. Then he couldn't help thinking about his friends chatting online without him. *If that business guy calls and the line is busy, he'll just call back later,* Carlos reasoned. *Or maybe the guy is too swamped to call tonight anyway. It'll just take a couple of minutes to see if any of my friends are online.*

Carlos wandered into the den, at first ignoring the tiny nudge of his conscience. Once he had logged on, though, he became uncomfortable. He knew his mom needed the information that the call would bring. He logged off and picked up a book. He knew he'd been right to follow his conscience when the telephone immediately rang and the machine picked up the message for his mom.

The closer you get to adulthood, the more obeying your parents can feel burdensome and unnecessary. Your parents have a God-given responsibility to guide you in the right direction as you grow. Your responsibility is to obey them. Obeying your parents, even in the little things, not only shows them the respect they deserve, it helps prepare you to obey other authority in your life—like the laws of man, and of course, the laws of God. Learning obedience will put you on the road to a healthier, happier, safer life.

Try this: *Obedience doesn't come naturally. It's a choice that gets easier the more often you obey. See for yourself how tough it can be to learn to obey. Try teaching a dog a trick. Or sit in on an obedience class at a nearby kennel. You'll soon see that obedience requires a conscious act of your will and a commitment to follow someone else's direction.*

Obey the Lord and you will live a long life, content and safe from harm.

Proverbs 19:23 GNT

Obey your parents in the Lord, for this is right.

Ephesians 6:1 NRSV

Obedience is the gateway through which knowledge, yes, and love, too, enter the mind.

Anne Sullivan

The Giving Heart

Give strength, give thought,

Give deeds, give wealth;

Give love, give tears

And give thyself.

Give, give, be always giving.

Who give not is not living;

The more you give,

The more you live.

Author Unknown

*Be generous, and you
will be prosperous. Help
others, and you will
be helped.*

— *Proverbs* 11:25 GNT

*Give to the poor and
you will never be in need.*

— *Proverbs* 28:27 GNT

THE TEST OF
GENEROSITY IS NOT
HOW MUCH YOU
GIVE, BUT HOW
MUCH YOU
HAVE LEFT.

AUTHOR UNKNOWN

Safe and Secure

The LORD will keep you safe. He will not let you fall into a trap.

~ *Proverbs 3:26* GNT

Her friends made it look so easy. Why couldn't Jen just get behind the wheel and drive? After all, she was sixteen. Friends, relatives, even the lady next door kept asking, "When are you getting your driver's license?"

Never! is what Jen wanted to shout back. She wasn't even sure why. Jen wanted the freedom of her own car, and she had her permit. As soon as Jen was in the driver's seat, though, her heart started racing, her palms started sweating, and she felt like an accident waiting to happen.

That's why it felt right when Jen's friend Carrie offered to pray with her about it. "Now picture God right there in the car with you," Jen's friend told her. After a while, Jen began to feel more confident. She could sense that God was helping her face whatever happened to be around the next corner.

Fear is a funny thing. It doesn't only strike when you're in danger. Sometimes it shows up for what seems like no reason at all. Whenever you feel afraid, no matter if what you're afraid of is big or small or something that seems like nothing at all, you can handle it. Why? God is always with you. Talking to him when you feel panic setting in not only calms your heart, but it also helps you put your fear into perspective. There is no storm he cannot calm.

Try this: *The next time you hear a scary story, notice how your body feels when you're afraid. Ask God to help calm your fears, even though you know what you're afraid of isn't real. Talk to God until you're no longer afraid. Then, do this the next time real fear takes hold.*

THE FEAR OF OTHERS LAYS A SNARE, BUT ONE WHO TRUSTS IN THE LORD IS SECURE.

PROVERBS 29:25
NRSV

LET US BE BOLD, THEN, AND SAY, "THE LORD IS MY HELPER. I WILL NOT BE AFRAID."

HEBREWS 13:6 GNT

Many of our fears are tissue paper-thin, and a single courageous step would carry us clear through them.

BRENDAN FRANCIS

Making Up

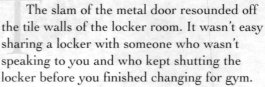

An ally offended is stronger than a city; such quarreling is like the bars of a castle.

~ *Proverbs* 18:19 NRSV

The slam of the metal door resounded off the tile walls of the locker room. It wasn't easy sharing a locker with someone who wasn't speaking to you and who kept shutting the locker before you finished changing for gym.

Gary worked the combination one more time as Dale gave him a final glare and headed off to the track. Gary had to admit that greeting his friend as "Dale the whale" probably wasn't the best way to say good morning—especially when he knew how touchy Dale was about his weight. It seemed funny at the time, but the good humor didn't last long. Dale had retaliated by pretending Gary didn't exist.

Just when they were becoming good friends, Gary blew it by making a careless, dumb remark. *I really like Dale*, Gary thought. *Maybe if I apologize we can get back on the right track.*

92

A relationship is like a window between two people. The closer you get, the wider the window slides open. When conflict arises, as it does in every relationship, the window slams shut. Without words of forgiveness and reconciliation, the window not only stays shut, but iron bars of bitterness drop into place, making the rebuilding of a relationship hard work. Relationships are worth fighting for, however. Don't let allies become enemies. Be the first one to say, "Let's make things right."

TRY THIS: *Draw a picture of a window between two hearts. Think about your most difficult relationship and write that name on one heart, your own on the other. Then think. How wide open is the window? Are there any bars holding it shut? What are some of the things you can do to help open the window wider? The next time you see this person, try out one of these thoughts and see how far the window opens.*

DO NOT FORGET YOUR FRIENDS OR YOUR FATHER'S FRIENDS.

PROVERBS 27:10 GNT

PEOPLE LEARN FROM ONE ANOTHER, JUST AS IRON SHARPENS IRON.

PROVERBS 27:17 GNT

A relationship is a living thing. It needs and benefits from the same attention to detail that an artist lavishes on his art.

DAVID VISCOTT

What Can I Do?

Whoever is kind to the poor lends to the LORD, and will be repaid in full.

~ *Proverbs 19:17* NRSV

What can you buy for a buck? A can of soda, less than half a burger at most drive-through restaurants, enough gas to drive around for maybe twenty minutes. A dollar doesn't go very far.

Did you know that 600 million children around the world live in families that get by on less than one dollar a day? That's not per person, that's for their entire family. Considering the population of the United States is under 250 million, that's a lot of people—kids just like you, except for the fact that they go to bed hungry almost every night.

God said that the poor will always be with us. That doesn't mean you should just be thankful you're not one of them and go on with your life. Have you heard the saying, "With privilege comes responsibility"? That means those with enough—often much more than enough—are responsible for sharing what they have with those in need.

There are many ways you and your family can reach out to the poor. Talk to your parents about supporting a child that lives in a distant country. Reach out to your own community by donating food and clothing to a nearby shelter. Churches in many cities collect specific items, such as powdered milk, canned good, or toiletries for their distribution. Better yet, make it really personal by helping someone you know who seems to be struggling.

Try this: Don't eat anything for one whole day—just drink plenty of juice and water. Be sure and talk to your parents about what you're doing and choose to fast on a day when you're not in school. When you find yourself thinking about how hungry you are, pray for the people who feel like this every day.

THOSE WHO ARE GENEROUS ARE BLESSED, FOR THEY SHARE THEIR BREAD WITH THE POOR.

PROVERBS 22:9 NRSV

BLESSED IS HE THAT CONSIDERETH THE POOR.

PSALM 41:1 KJV

Not to enable the poor to share in our goods is to steal from them and deprive them of life.

SAINT JOHN CHRYSOSTOM

Owning Up

The LORD gave us mind and conscience; we cannot hide from ourselves.
~ *Proverbs* 20:27 GNT

A GOOD
CONSCIENCE IS A
MINE OF WEALTH.
—SAINT BERNARD
OF CLAIRVAUX

Sam got back into the driver's seat and just sat there. If he pulled out and moved the truck to another spot, no one would ever know. The front bumper on his dad's truck looked fine. It was the bumper on the back of the dark blue convertible parked next to him that was crumpled like an old homework assignment.

"I hate parking," Sam muttered to himself. Driving was a breeze, but squeezing his dad's old pickup into a parking space was a challenge. He thought he'd done it right this time—that is, until he heard that horrible crunching noise.

Sam knew what could happen if he owned up to what he'd done. He'd have to apologize to the owner of the convertible. His insurance would go up. He'd have to use his own money to help pay for the damages. If he drove away, Sam would only have to figure out was how to live with himself. But he knew the right decision and made it. He would accept the consequences.

Taking care of your conscience is like taking care of your room. When it's clean and everything is in place, you can relax. If you only give it the appearance of being clean by shoving things under the bed, you have to be on guard. Mom still might see it when she comes in. When you do something wrong, whether accidentally or intentionally, your conscience reacts in a similar way. You can't hide your misbehavior. The only way to clear your conscience is by accepting the consequences of your actions and making things right.

Try this: Put something in the middle of the floor, like a chair or a stack of books. Leave it there for the next week. Every time you bump into it or have to walk around it, ask God to bring to mind anything you need to clean up off the floor of your conscience. Act on what comes to mind.

WHO CAN SAY, "I HAVE KEPT MY HEART PURE; I AM CLEAN AND WITHOUT SIN"?

PROVERBS 20:9 NIV

KEEP YOUR FAITH AND A CLEAR CONSCIENCE.

1 TIMOTHY 1:19 GNT

Conscience tells us in our innermost being of the presence of God and of the moral difference between good and evil.

BILLY GRAHAM

The Forgiving Heart

The truest joys they seldom prove,

Who free from quarrels live;

'Tis the most tender part of love.

Each other to forgive.

John Sheffield

Forgive us the wrongs we have done, as we forgive the wrongs that others have done to us.

— *Matthew 6:12* GNT

Be kind to one another, tenderhearted, forgiving one another, as God in Christ has forgiven you.

— *Ephesians 4:32* NRSV

FORGIVENESS IS THE KEY THAT UNLOCKS THE DOOR OF RESENTMENT AND THE HANDCUFFS OF HATE.

CORRIE TEN BOOM

Front and Center

Hot tempers cause arguments, but patience brings peace.

~ *Proverbs* 15:18 GNT

Being chosen drum major for the marching band wasn't a surprise for Jason—or for anyone who knew him. Musical talent, innate rhythm, and self-confidence were as natural to him as breathing. Jason knew he could lead Westin's school band to the finals.

But there were challenges already. Vince, the only trombone player, just wasn't getting the drill. When the band turned left, Vince inevitably went the opposite direction. It was only their first week of practice, but Jason could feel his impatience growing to the breaking point. "Vince. Front and center." Jason shouted. "Learn your right from your left or join the chess club."

The band members stopped mid-step and looked at Vince, whose face was red with embarrassment. Jason regretted his impatient words. He knew he had not acted like a good leader or a good Christian. After practice ended, Jason apologized to Vince and offered to help him with the routines outside of practice time.

Patience is a virtue that grows stronger through practice. You have an opportunity to practice patience every time you're asked to forebear with mistakes and shortcomings—those of others as well as your own. Every time you adjust to unexpected circumstances, you have a chance to see your patience grow. When your faith is tried, your love tested, your kindness stretched, your expectations diverted, God has provided you with all you need to nourish the virtue of patience in your life.

TRY THIS: *The next time you're in the grocery store, practice patience by purposefully choosing to wait in the longest line instead of the shortest. Look at each person in front of you as someone God loves rather than as someone who is hindering your time schedule. Whisper a prayer for each individual. When impatience sneaks up on you in the future, put this same practice into action.*

A MAN'S WISDOM GIVES HIM PATIENCE; IT IS TO HIS GLORY TO OVERLOOK AN OFFENSE.

PROVERBS 19:11 NIV

IF WE HOPE FOR WHAT WE DO NOT SEE, WE WAIT FOR IT WITH PATIENCE.

ROMANS 8:25 NRSV

Patience is power; with time and patience the mulberry leaf becomes silk.

ANCIENT PROVERB

SHOULD'VE BEEN ME

Peace of mind makes the body healthy.

~ Proverbs 14:30 GNT

As Angela walked into the biology room, Kaley could feel her muscles tense and her blood pressure rise. *Angela gets all the breaks, Kaley thought, including what should have been my spot on the varsity swim team.* Even though they'd been friends for years, Kaley had told Angela exactly how she felt last week, right after the coach had announced the squad members. Things had been uncomfortably quiet between them ever since.

But today, Angela stopped beside Kaley's desk. "I really am sorry you didn't make the team," Angela said. "But can't you just be happy for me? I would be happy for you."

"I am happy for you," Kaley responded, and realized she meant it. Immediately her muscles relaxed and her blood pressure returned to normal. Inside, she was thinking, I can't let envy spoil our friendship. From that day on, Kaley could be found in the stands at every swim meet cheering for her friend Angela.

Envy can destroy friendships. It can also tear away at your self-esteem by causing you to focus on others and overlook your own unique gifts and talents. You can lose the joy of being who you are and become defined by who you are not. Why let envy steal from you? When you catch yourself thinking *It should've been me*, immediately ask God to adjust your attitude until you can say "I'm happy for you" and mean it.

Try this: *When you find yourself feeling envious of someone, purchase a greeting card for that person. It can even be just an attractive, blank note card. Ask God to help you write a note congratulating that person on his or her achievement, opportunity, or even new possession. Then, hand deliver it.*

WHERE THERE IS JEALOUSY AND SELFISHNESS, THERE IS ALSO DISORDER.

James 3:16 GNT

WE MUST NOT BE PROUD OR IRRITATE ONE ANOTHER OR BE JEALOUS OF ONE ANOTHER.

Galatians 5:26 GNT

Envy's memory is nothing but a row of hooks to hang up grudges on.

JOHN WATSON FOSTER

Choose to Smile

A cheerful look brings joy to the heart.

~ *Proverbs* 15:30 *NIV*

WONDROUS IS THE STRENGTH OF CHEERFULNESS, AND ITS POWER OF ENDURANCE.
—THOMAS CARLYLE

Going from gloomy to cheerful usually doesn't happen in a matter of minutes, but there is something you can do to encourage the process along. Research has shown that forcing yourself to smile when you're feeling down can actually make you feel happier.

Putting on a smile can be a big help. Odds are it will take additional strategies to maintain a cheerful outlook through the roller-coaster ups and downs of life. One of these strategies would be to take a spiritual attitude adjustment—a determination to ditch the gloom and focus on the good things, the funny things, the uplifting things God has placed in your life. Ask God to help you identify and replace negative patterns of thought with positive ones.

If you find it too difficult to capture and maintain an attitude of cheerfulness, you may need to ask your parents or a trusted counselor to help you evaluate why being cheerful is a struggle for you.

Cheerfulness has many benefits. It can improve your relationships with others and even enhance your body's ability to ward off sickness. It sets a positive tone or perspective through which you can view the world. No wonder God encourages cheerfulness in his children's lives. Practice looking for the good all around you and focusing your thoughts on your blessings. And, of course, don't forget to smile.

Try this: *For the next few mornings, take two minutes in front of the bathroom mirror to practice your smile. Try different poses — lips closed, teeth showing, nose crinkled up. Don't hesitate to laugh at yourself. When you have a couple of good smiles down, put them on in front of others.*

BEING CHEERFUL
KEEPS YOU HEALTHY.

PROVERBS 17:22 GNT

A GLAD HEART
MAKES A CHEERFUL
COUNTENANCE.

PROVERBS 15:13
NRSV

Cheerfulness, like spring, opens all the blossoms of the inward man.

JEAN PAUL RICHTER

SHOULD'VE KNOWN BETTER

The lips of the wise protect them.

— *Proverbs* 14:3 NRSV

"Hey, looks like there's finally a girl worth looking at in this school." Garth said loudly as the new senior who'd transferred from across town carried her lunch past their table. The new girl didn't respond, but Heather stood up abruptly, grabbed her tray, and, with a hurried "Got to go," disappeared into the crowded cafeteria.

Garth raised his eyebrow and continued eating his burger. Parker cleared his throat, and then said quietly, "If you haven't noticed, Heather happens to be a girl in this school. Since she hangs around with us so much, she may seem like just one of the guys, but she's not."

Garth tried to laugh off the reprimand. It was just a careless comment. But Garth knew he'd see Heather in his next class. He'd have to say something. *This time*, Garth thought, *I'll figure out what I'm going to say before I open my mouth.*

106

Chances are your foot will occasionally wind up in your mouth. But repeated carelessness with your words is a bad habit that can cost you your reputation and ruin your relationships. The good news is that it's a habit you can change with God's help. Ask him to help you replace sarcastic, offhand remarks with honest words of encouragement. Ask him to help you think through your opinions before you share them with others.

TRY THIS: *Pay attention to the words that come out of your mouth. At the end of each day, grade yourself on a 10-point scale. Decide if your words were more helpful (1–5) or more hurtful (6–10). Record your score for one week. If you're not happy with the result, ask God to help you turn it around.*

IF YOU WANT TO STAY OUT OF TROUBLE, BE CAREFUL WHAT YOU SAY.

PROVERBS 21:23 GNT

HOW FORCIBLE ARE RIGHT WORDS!

JOB 6:25 KJV

Handle them carefully, for words have more power than atom bombs.

PEARL STRACHAN

"Hope" is the thing with feathers—

That perches in the soul—

And sings the tunes without the words—

And never stops—at all.

Emily Dickinson

The hope of the righteous ends in gladness.

— *Proverbs* 10:28 NRSV

Surely there is a future, and your hope will not be cut off.

— *Proverbs* 23:18 NRSV

IF YOU DO NOT HOPE, YOU WILL NOT FIND OUT WHAT IS BEYOND YOUR HOPES.

CLEMENT OF ALEXANDRIA

Dangerous Games

Wise people see danger and go to a safe place.

— *Proverbs* 27:12 *NIRV*

IF YOU PLAY
WITH FIRE, YOU
GET BURNED.
—ENGLISH
PROVERB

Chelsea and her friend Jenny had been flattered when Amy, one of the most popular girls in school, asked them if they'd like to come over to her house after school and hang out with her and her friends. It had been fun at first, sitting around in Amy's room laughing and talking. Everything changed, though, when one of the girls suggested they play truth or dare and Jenny had chosen to go with the dare.

"Open these and chug them as fast as you can" said Amy, pulling a six-pack of beer out from under her bed. "We dare you to drink at least three."

That was it for Chelsea. "Let's go," she told Jenny. "These people aren't our friends."

Chelsea and Jenny could hear the girls laughing as they headed down the stairs. But they knew that even if everyone in the whole school was laughing, it wasn't worth putting themselves in danger.

Turning away from doing what you know is wrong isn't always easy, especially if you have an audience. But there is always one person who applauds the wise choices you make—God. Every time you turn away from things that can harm you physically, mentally, or spiritually, you are turning toward your loving Father. He always has your best interest at heart. When you feel like you're the only one backing away from danger, realize that God is by your side.

TRY THIS: *Suggest to two or three of your friends that you get together to discuss those activities that you feel are dangerous—riding with someone who has been drinking, for example. Agree to be accountable to each other in those areas. Get together at least once a month to discuss how you're doing with your commitments.*

DISCRETION WILL PROTECT YOU, AND UNDERSTANDING WILL GUARD YOU.

PROVERBS 2:11 NIV

PURSUE RIGHTEOUSNESS, FAITH, LOVE AND PEACE, ALONG WITH THOSE WHO CALL ON THE LORD OUT OF A PURE HEART.

2 TIMOTHY 2:22 NIV

Out of this nettle, danger, we pluck this flower, safety.

WILLIAM SHAKESPEARE

WHEN IT COUNTS

What is desirable in a person is loyalty.

~ *Proverbs 19:22* NRSV

I WOULD BE
TRUE, FOR THERE
ARE THOSE WHO
TRUST ME.
—HOWARD A.
WALTER

Volleyball was Carmen's life—at least that's how it seemed. Now that women's volleyball was over, and the championship trophy was theirs, she was eagerly anticipating the men's championship final that evening and the party that would follow.

Maybe she and Kurt, the team's captain, would get some time to talk at the party. Maybe he'd even ask her out. As Carmen headed out the door, she hurriedly picked up the ringing phone. Kayla's shaking voice made Carmen stop and listen. "Don't pick me up," Kayla said through tears. "I can't— I don't feel like going tonight."

Carmen was torn. She'd looked forward this night all week. But she and Kayla had been friends for years, and she knew the problems Kayla had been having with some of the kids at school. There would be other games, other chances to talk to Kurt, but Kayla needed her now. Carmen knew where she should be.

You probably have someone in your life for whom you feel a deep sense of loyalty. If so, you know that "I'll be there for you" doesn't mean "I'll support you when it fits into my schedule." Being loyal means you'll be there even when it costs you, even when it's inconvenient, even when it hurts. And being loyal in your relationship with the Lord is important too. He says he will always be by your side, loving you, protecting you. Will you be there for him?

Try this: Think of the ways people have shown their loyalty to you in the past. Then, write a thank-you note to one of those people. Tell that person how much his or her loyalty has meant to you. Don't forget to take a moment to thank God for bringing that special person into your life.

He who pursues righteousness and loyalty finds life, righteousness and honor.

Proverbs 21:21
NASB

The faithfulness of the Lord endures forever.

Psalm 117:2 NRSV

Loyalty means nothing unless it has at its heart the absolute principle of self-sacrifice.

Woodrow Wilson

Search My Heart

Human ways are under the eyes of the LORD, and he examines all their paths.

~ *Proverbs* 5:21 *NRSV*

REASON DECEIVES
US; CONSCIENCE,
NEVER.
—JEAN JACQUES
ROUSSEAU

If Conner didn't get his research paper on the Italian Renaissance finished by this evening, his World History grade was going down. He sighed and went back to the Internet to find a few more facts on Michelangelo. But the site that popped up on his screen was far from Renaissance art. At first he was stunned, then intrigued. Most of all, he felt guilty. He guessed the software his parents had installed didn't filter out all of the many sites they'd hoped.

Flashing at the bottom of the screen, there was a link to another site. Maybe he would just take a peek. He tried telling himself that he did need a break from studying and that if anything really bad showed upon the screen, he's just turn it off. *But what if my parents find out?* Conner asked himself. *I guess if I'm afraid they'll find out, I shouldn't be doing it in the first place,* he reasoned.

It's not a good idea, but it is possible to keep some of the things you do from your parents. You can forget about trying to keep them from God, though. He sees everything—not just your actions, but also the thoughts and intentions of your heart. That's a good thing. Once you know he's watching, it will be easier to keep your heart clean and pure. You won't fall for the old justification, "No one will know." A clean heart is a treasure far more valuable than gold.

Try this: Work out your own rating system for determining whether something is worthy of your time and mind, for example: G for Good, PG for Pretty Good, R for Risky, and X for Extraordinarily Bad. When an activity comes up, rate it. If it rates a G or a PG, you are fine. Anything less should get an instant no.

Those who are good are rewarded here on earth.

Proverbs 11:31 GNT

The good person out of the good treasure of the heart produces good.

Luke 6:45 NRSV

Conscience is the inner voice that warns us that someone might be looking.

H. L. Mencken

Payback Time

Do not say, "I'll pay you back for this wrong!" Wait for the LORD, and he will deliver you.

— *Proverbs 20:22 NIV*

Somewhere between "once upon a time" and "happily ever after," most fairy tales include a chapter that could be called "payback time." This is where the evil stepsisters are forced into servitude, the grandmother-eating wolf is killed by the noble woodsman, or the dastardly captain of the pirate ship is gobbled up by a crocodile. The villains get what they deserve. And that's what makes fairy tales "fair."

Real life, on the other hand, doesn't seem fair at all. When you get cut off on the freeway, the other driver rarely ends up getting a ticket—he gets to his destination before you. And when one of your classmates makes fun of the way you look, she doesn't grow a wart on her nose—she's more likely to be voted prom queen. You feel as though you can't live a fairy tale life, unless you set things right. But the truth is, that job belongs to God, who is the ultimate author of the story.

Your life isn't a fairy tale, but it is similar in that you will experience situations that aren't fair and people who aren't kind. God has a radical set of guidelines for dealing with those who treat you badly. He asks you to love them, forgive them, and leave the chapter on payback time for him to write. Amazingly, the Bible lists no exceptions to the leave-vengeance-to-God rule. No matter how grievous the offense, God's instruction is clear.

Try this: *Write an outline for a fairy tale where you are the hero or heroine. Let the villain do his worst, but figure out how you can show love in spite of what the villain does to you. Then share your fairy tale by telling it to a younger brother, sister, or family friend.*

Do not repay evil for evil or abuse for abuse; but, on the contrary, repay with a blessing.

1 Peter 3:9 NRSV

Do not repay anyone evil for evil.

Romans 12:17 NRSV

Revenge is sweet but forgiveness is sweeter.
Author Unknown

The Righteous Heart

My hope is built on nothing less
Than Jesus' blood and righteousness.
I dare not trust the sweetest frame,
But wholly trust in Jesus' Name.
When He shall come with trumpet sound
Oh, may I then in Him be found;
Dressed in His righteousness alone,
Faultless to stand before the throne.

Edward Mote

*Blessings are on the
head of the righteous.*

— *Proverbs 10:6* NRSV

*In the way of
righteousness is life; and
in the pathway thereof
there is no death.*

— *Proverbs 12:28* KJV

THE MOST
IMPORTANT
INGREDIENT OF
RIGHTEOUSNESS IS
TO RENDER TO
GOD THE SERVICE
AND HOMAGE DUE
TO HIM.

JOHN CALVIN

Helping Out

Show me someone who does a good job, and I will show you someone who is better than most and worthy of the company of kings.

~ *Proverbs* 22:29 GNT

WORK IS THE
MEAT OF LIFE,
PLEASURE THE
DESSERT.
—PETER F. DRUCKER

From the street, Mrs. Jordan's house looked abandoned. Its once-white paint had long since peeled, exposing mottled gray timber. Recent spring rains had pushed the overgrown weeds to where they almost obscured the front porch. Dillon picked up his hoe and went to work.

"Wish I could give you a little something for all your work," Mrs. Jordan said apologetically. "Best I can do is a glass of cold water and a few cookies."

"Thanks, Mrs. Jordan," Dillon replied. "Don't worry about it. I enjoy helping you out."

It wasn't that Dillon loved battling weeds. But he did care about Mrs. Jordan, and, more than that, Dillon loved God. Whenever Dillon was tackling an unpleasant task, he just pictured himself working in God's garden, washing God's dishes, or painting God's porch. It not only made the job more pleasant, but it encouraged him to do his very best. Dillon finished off his glass of water and got back to work.

On any given day, the work you perform may be an act of kindness, a family responsibility, or the basis for your paycheck. God knows that your daily tasks fall into many categories. In every case, he asks only two things—that you commit your work to him and that you do the best job you possibly can. Approaching your work in that way changes it from drudgery to blessing. It endows the simplest task with eternal purpose.

TRY THIS: *When you begin a task, hesitate long enough to whisper a prayer to God. "Heavenly Father, I commit this task to you. Please give me the self-discipline I need to stay with it until it is finished and the determination to do my best." Thank God for the opportunity to do your work for his glory.*

MANUAL LABOR HAS ITS REWARD.

PROVERBS 12:14
NRSV

IN ALL TOIL THERE IS PROFIT.

PROVERBS 14:23
NRSV

Work becomes worship when done for the Lord.

AUTHOR UNKOWN

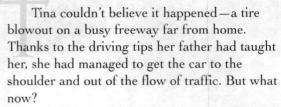

HE'S ALWAYS LISTENING

The prayer of the upright is God's delight.

— *Proverbs 15:8 NRSV*

Tina couldn't believe it happened—a tire blowout on a busy freeway far from home. Thanks to the driving tips her father had taught her, she had managed to get the car to the shoulder and out of the flow of traffic. But what now?

For a few minutes, Tina just sat there, watching the cars race past, regretting that she had left her cell phone on the kitchen counter at home. Finally, she remembered the other thing her father had taught her. She began to talk to God. "I don't know what to do, Lord. Please send someone to help me out of this jam."

Tina had barely finished speaking when she saw the rotating lights of a police car pulling up behind her. The officer told her to stay put while he called for a tow truck. An hour later, with her tire replaced, she was whispering a prayer of thanks as she headed home.

Tina didn't need a cell phone to ask for God's help. He was right there with her. Before she even said the words, help was on the way. That is the power of prayer—an ever-present connection with almighty God. No matter where you go, your prayers will reach God. No matter what you ask, your prayers are never too big for God. No matter who you are, God is listening.

Try this: Begin a prayer journal. Write the date at the top of the page, and write down those requests you have made of God that day. When God answers a prayer you've prayed, go back to the page where you recorded it and write "Answered," along with the date. Soon you will have solid evidence of God's intervention in your life.

THE LORD HEARS THE PRAYER OF THE RIGHTEOUS.

PROVERBS 15:29
NRSV

SPEND A LOT OF TIME IN PRAYER. ALWAYS BE WATCHFUL AND THANKFUL.

COLOSSIANS 4:2
NIRV

The more you pray, the easier it becomes. The easier it becomes, the more you will pray.

MOTHER TERESA

The Wise Heart

A wise old owl
sat on an oak.
The more he saw
the less he spoke;
The less he spoke
the more he heard;
Why aren't we like
that wise old bird?

Edward Hersey Richards

Love wisdom, and she will make you great. Embrace her, and she will bring you honor.

~ *Proverbs* 4:8 GNT

Those who become wise are happy; wisdom will give them life.

~ *Proverbs* 3:18 GNT

The next best thing to being wise oneself is to live in a circle of those who are.

C. S. Lewis

Other books in the Proverbs for Life™ series:

Proverbs for Life™ for Men
Proverbs for Life™ for You
Proverbs for Life™ for Women

All available from your favorite bookstore.
We would like to hear from you.
Please send your comments about this book to:

Inspirio™, the gift group of Zondervan
Attn: Product Development
Grand Rapids, Michigan 49530

www.inspirio.com

Our mission:
*To provide distinctively Christian gifts that point people to God's Word
through refreshing messages and innovative designs.*

inspirio™
The gift group of Zondervan